Jesus, My All in All
Symbols

Activity Book and Teacher's Guide

Ida Irene Stiles-Brown

Illustrated by Ida Lee Hodge

TEACH Services, Inc.
PUBLISHING
www.TEACHServices.com • (800) 367-1844

World rights reserved. This book or any portion thereof may not be copied or reproduced in any form or manner whatever, except as provided by law, without the written permission of the publisher, except by a reviewer who may quote brief passages in a review.

The author assumes full responsibility for the accuracy of all facts and quotations as cited in this book. The opinions expressed in this book are the author's personal views and interpretations, and do not necessarily reflect those of the publisher.

This book is provided with the understanding that the publisher is not engaged in giving spiritual, legal, medical, or other professional advice. If authoritative advice is needed, the reader should seek the counsel of a competent professional.

Copyright © 2021 Ida Irene Stiles-Brown

Copyright © 2021 TEACH Services, Inc.

ISBN-13: 978-1-4796-1191-1 (Paperback)

ISBN-13: 978-1-4796-1192-8 (ePub)

Scripture references are taken from the King James Version (KJV) of the Bible. Public domain.

This material is reproducible for use in the home and in the classroom in connection with *Jesus, My All in All, Symbols*, children's book. The printable material is meant to supplement the hands-on activities and projects. Children learn best when they are in God's nature, exploring the world He has given us. As we connect God's Word with nature, which points us to our Creator, the children will understand the concepts with the help of the Holy Spirit.

There are several activities, crafts, and game ideas in each section. They do not have to be used all at once. You can pick and choose those that fit your group to best get the information across.

There are many wonderful reasons to use the King James Version of the Bible. One of the reasons is to lift up the vocabulary of the child. Reading the Word of God in the poetic form of the King James Version will increase the child's reading and vocabulary skills as the parent or teacher teaches them how to find the definitions of unknown words in a dictionary. You do this as you would when reading any other book. Teaching children to look up an unfamiliar word also teaches them how to use a concordance, which in turn expands their Bible study skills. The definition of the words that have been picked for the vocabulary section have been taken from the Strong's Concordance.

Acknowledgments

To God be the glory for the great things He has done. These are the people He has chosen to be His hands and feet for this book. A special thanks to my grandmother, Ida Hodge, for working tirelessly on the pictures while on oxygen in the middle of her heart procedures. I also want to thank Matt and Emily Anderson for making this workbook possible through their support and encouragement. Another couple who was integral in the progression of *Jesus, My All in All, Symbols* reading book was Sophia and Gary Rayner. A big thank you to everyone for their support and prayers. As always, my beloved family deserves extra hugs for the time sacrificed to make it possible.

Table of Contents

Lesson 1: Can the Young Speak?..11
    Activity 1—Grabbing Hold of God's Strength...11
    Activity 2—Why Do Christians Still Have Trials?..12
    In Nature 1 (Spring/Summer)—God of the Impossible 13
    Learn How the Lord Will Prepare You for a Great Work! 15
    Get to Know Great Young People of the Bible 16
    Coloring Page..17
    Coloring Page..18
    Vocabulary Activities..19
    Writing a Short Essay 21
    Answer Key for Lesson 1 24

Lesson 2: Angel of the Lord 25
    Activity 1—Different Names 25
    Activity 2—Darkness and Fear..26
    Activity 3—Nature Walk 27
    Word Scramble—Other Names or Symbols for Jesus...28
    Define 29
    Coloring Page..30
    Bookmark 31
    Answer Key for Lesson 2 33
    Coloring Page..34

Lesson 3: The Covenant 35
    Activity 1—Refracting Light..35
    Activity 2—Color Wheel 35
    Practicing Dictionary Use 37

    Word Scramble—A Promise through Clothes 38

    Multiple Choice—The Covenant 39

    Answer Key for Lesson 3 41

Lesson 4: Testament 42

    Activity 1—Built on the Rock 42

    Activity 2—Red Rover 43

    Coded Words Puzzle 44

    Acts of the Promise 45

    Answer Key for Lesson 4 46

Lesson 5: The Law 47

    Activity 1—Law of Gravity 47

    Basic Meaning of the Law 49

    Synonyms 50

    Breaking down the Text 51

    Character 53

    Answer Key for Lesson 5 54

    Coloring Page 57

Lesson 6: Prophecy 58

    Activity 1—Prophecy through Nature 58

    Activity 2—Prophecy Revealing the Unseen 59

    Crossword Puzzle 60

    Coloring Page 62

    Prophecy Short Answer 63

    Answer Key for Lesson 6 64

Lesson 7: Meat 66

    Activity 1—All Have Sinned 66

    The Bible Explains Itself 68

    Meat in Action 69

    Coloring Page 70

    Writing a Short Essay 71

    Answer Key for Lesson 7 73

Lesson 8: Gospel 74
    Activity 1—Noticing Sin in Nature 74
    Activity 2—Missing the Mark 74
    Activity 3—Mark and Reflection 75
    More to the Gospel 77
    Multiple Choice—Known by Love 78
    Coloring Page 79
    Metal Tooling 80
    Answer Key for Lesson 8 82

Can the Young Speak?

Lesson 1

A Note to Parents and Teachers:

This section is to help children feel empowered and confident that the Lord can and will use children for His work. We want them to have faith in this idea, in hopes that it will lead them to have a desire to do great things for the Lord. My prayer is that this desire will foster an obedient heart that can prepare them to be used. These activities are to help the mind to understand how God gives us strength, but to also know that with any great task comes great responsibility.

Activity 1

Grabbing Hold of God's Strength

Prayer: Pray before each activity. Ask the Father for His Spirit to guide the minds of the students to learn more about Him and their Savior, Jesus Christ.

Items needed: four volunteers (one of the volunteers should be a smaller child while the other three are slightly bigger)

Have two children stand about 3 yards apart from each other. One will represent the starting point while the other will represent the ending point. The other two volunteers are going to stand at the starting point. Then ask the smaller child to pick up the larger child and carry them to the end point. This should be difficult; in fact, the child should not be able to do it. The task should seem impossible.

Scripting: Explain to the children that sometimes in life the task that is set before us can seem impossible and too difficult to do. But with God all things are possible. Even though we are little, we can do great things for Him because He is so big and mighty. We must allow the Lord to lead and grab hold of His strength, and when we do that, the impossible becomes possible. How do we grab hold of the strength of our Maker?

1. Prayer (James 1:5)
2. Reading our Bible (Prov. 2:3–6, John 15:7)
3. Seeking advice from a godly person (Prov. 11:14)

4. Singing (Ps. 59:16, 17)
5. Joy (Neh. 8:10)
6. Obedience (Deut. 11:8; Ps. 103:20)
7. Trust (Isa. 30:15)

Explain: I (the teacher) represent one of the items that we mentioned that gives us the Lord's strength (prayer, reading Bible, etc.).

Now lock arms with the younger child and make a cradle or seat. Have the older child sit on your hands/arms, with most of the weight on you as the adult, and carry the older child to the end point, working as a team with the younger child.

Scripting: Explain how this shows God's strength when we lock arms with Him, and He then can work with us to accomplish the task. What does it mean to lock arms with God? What does it look like? Some may say pray, read your Bible, or believe in His Word. These are all good answers.

Activity 2

Why Do Christians Still Have Trials?

Set up an obstacle course for the children and make it somewhat hard for their age group. The goal is for it to be challenging, but easy enough that they can improve their time and skills as they go through the course again.

Question: Before children start the course, ask them: **Why do Christians have trials?** If the children can't come up with any answers, move directly to the obstacle course. If they come up with Biblical answers, thank them for sharing, move to the course and allow the information to sink in for the rest of the children.

Obstacle Course: Have all children run through the course once and record each person's time, but don't tell them you are recording their time (God does not always tell us when we are being challenged until we are in the situation). After each person has gone through, tell the kids they are going to get to do the course again. Record each child's time without them knowing. Hopefully, they have improved their time; if not, there will be another application to show this.

Discussion: Have children come together in a group and ask them: **What does this obstacle course tell us about the trials Christians go through**? They might say trials can be like an obstacle course—kind of hard; trials are challenging; trials show you areas in which you are weak. Affirm their answers if they are on track with the idea that an obstacle course can be hard just like a trial. Ask: **Do you think the trials make you better or stronger? Why or why not?** Some may say yes, while others may say no. Try to find out if they are saying no because they don't like the trials, therefore they don't think they make them stronger. **Share** Bible texts on why we have trials and how it is to make us stronger and to glorify God (Ps. 107:41–43; Isa. 48:10; 1 Peter 1:7; 4:12–14; Rom. 5:3–4; James 1:3–4, 12). **At this point share with them their results for the obstacle course.** It might be better to share just the improvements in time for each individual instead of the overall course time. This will help to avoid competition among the children, where they will lose sight of the theme. The idea is for self-growth, not competition with each other. **Explain** how trials can make us grow, and with each trial we become stronger only when we grasp hold of the Lord's strength. We don't always know we are being tried, until we are in the situation and fail. Failure isn't always bad; it helps to remind us of our weaknesses and where we need to grow in the Lord more. Even though trials are hard, and I don't like them either, I know that the Lord allows such things to make me stronger in Him. He has said when I am weak, He is strong (2 Cor. 12:9), and I can do all things in Christ who strengthens me (Phil. 4:13). Just remember this promise if you think the trial is too much for you: the Lord does not test us beyond what we can handle (1 Cor. 10:13). When we are feeling like the trial is too hard, claim that promise and also run to the Word of God, because we are told it will comfort us (Ps. 119:50). We are also told that when the Law of the Lord is our delight, then it will also help us when we are afflicted (Ps. 119:92). Remember to grab hold of the strength of the Lord.

What are ways we can grab hold of the Lord's strength?

1. Prayer (James 1:5)
2. Reading our Bible (Prov. 2:3–6, John 15:7)
3. Seeking advice from a godly person (Prov. 11:14)
4. Singing (Ps. 59:16, 17)
5. Joy (Neh. 8:10)
6. Obedience (Deut. 11:8; Ps. 103:20)
7. Trust (Isa. 30:15)

Final obstacle course and final discussion: Finish by doing the obstacle course again. Now the kids will probably be even more motivated to beat their time. **At the end of this third round announce the improvements for each individual. If they did considerably better ask them**: Why? They will probably say it is because they knew they were being timed. Tell them: **You now know that the Lord will allow you to have trials. Put forth your best effort to run the obstacle course of life, with your best effort in grabbing hold of the Lord's strength.**

In Nature 1 (Spring/Summer)

God of the Impossible

Discussions as you walk:

Take the kids out for a nature walk. Look at the insects, birds, flowers, etc. and ask the children how they reveal the Creator.

You can also ask how we can see the hand of sin on the earth as well, i.e.: when you pick a flower it will die; a bird will eat an insect, and it is no more. We can also see the hand of sin because many animals are afraid of humans; we can't go and pet a wild bird but can only hear its song.

Talk about how wonderful it will be in heaven where we can not only enjoy the earth made new, but we do not have to worry about bugs biting us and animals being afraid of us.

Activity: See if the children can find a bumblebee. If there aren't any in your area, you can enjoy the nature walk looking for one while bringing a picture of a bee along with you so the children are able to have a visual when it comes to the discussion.

Have children gather around you while sitting in the grass or at a picnic table.

Scripting: Show picture of bumblebee and ask: **What is this?** Bee. **What do you notice about this insect?** Children might say: a little fuzzy, has 6 legs, yellow and black. **What do you notice about the body to wing proportion?** Children might say that the body is big while the wings are small.

Discussion: Talk to the children about how it has often been said that a bee shouldn't be able to fly, because the size of his body is too big compared to his wing size. If this were true, then it would be an illustration of how God wants to use you. The task the Lord may have for you may seem too big for your wing size. You may feel as if you are too small to do such a big task, but remember the Father is with you. How is He with you? Through prayer, His word, His Spirit, in song etc. The strength of the wings may seem too small for the bee to fly, but yet it does. Our strength is small, but the strength of the Lord is infinite. Grab hold of His strength and you will soar. (May need to review on page 13 how to grab hold of the Lord's strength.) When we grab hold of the Lord's strength, what seems impossible is possible; we can soar when no one thought we could.

It used to be considered a fact that the bumblebee should not be able to fly and that it defied the law of physics. Because of modern technology, scientists have discovered God's design. Even though the wings are too small for a bee to fly when flapped up and down, the bee can fly because of a sweeping motion. This causes a current of air to flow in a whirl-pooling fashion, causing flight for this insect. This insight gives us a great lesson on soaring with the Lord. Many times we try to do things with our own strength, and we may lift off the ground a bit, but in order to really fly we might need to change our wing action in a different direction. For example, if we are focusing on our ideas and strength, we don't see long-lasting success. We may feel that we are flying for a bit of time, but then we fall we crash. If we change our wing direction and grab hold of the Lord's strength first (can review page 13), our take-off may be slow, but we will be in the air longer. Continue to walk in nature, allowing the children to ponder what has been discussed.

You can hear a little more on how a bee flies by listening to Michael Dickinson during his Ted Talk at: https://1ref.us/1of (accessed March 30, 2021)

I would not recommend letting your children watch it because he makes comments about evolution. My recommendation is to glean the factual, scientific information on flight and relay that to the children.

Learn How the Lord Will Prepare You for a Great Work!

Fill in the blanks to find the answers to the following questions.

1. **How can you overcome the world?** 1 John 5:4

For whatsoever is _____ ____ _____ overcometh the world: and this is the _____ that overcometh the world, *even* our _____ .

2. **Who can overcome the world?** 1 John 5:5

Who is he that overcometh the world, but he that _____ that _____ is the _____ of _____ ?

3. **How can you do hard things for God?** Luke 17:6

And the Lord said, If ye had _____ as a grain of _____ _____, ye might say unto this sycamine tree, Be thou _____ up by the root, and be thou planted in the _____ ; and it should obey you.

4. **Can we ask anything we want of the Lord and He will do it?** 1 John 5:14

And this is the _____ that we have in him, that, if we ask any thing _____ to his _____ , he heareth us:

5. **How do we know God's will and what do we have faith in?** Romans 10:17

So then _____ *cometh* by _____ , and _____ by the _____ of God.

Get to Know Great Young People of the Bible

The Lord used the following young people to do great things in the lives of others. Write the letter next to the name in order to match the person with his accomplishment. Consider reading these stories with your class or parent, and when finished, then try the matching activity.

____	1. Josiah (2 Kings 22:1–20; 23:1–4)	a. Would not bow down to an idol.
____	2. Daniel (Daniel 2:1–49)	b. Chosen to be the mother of the King.
____	3. Little Maid (2 Kings 5:1–14)	c. Was a teenager when given dreams of the future
____	4. Jeremiah (Jeremiah 1:1–10)	d. Took all the idols out of the temple and burned them.
____	5. Mary (Luke 1:26–38)	e. Working in the temple when God called him.
____	6. Hananiah, Mishael, Azariah (Daniel 3:1–30)	f. Gave an interpretation of a dream.
____	7. Samuel (1 Samuel 3:1–15)	g. Master was healed from leprosy.
____	8. Joseph (Genesis 37:4–11)	h. God anointed his lips to be a speaker to the people of God.

"If ye have faith as a grain of mustard seed, ye shall say unto this mountain, Remove hence to yonder place; and it shall remove; and nothing shall be impossible unto you" (Matt. 17:20).

"And the Lord said, If ye had faith as a grain of mustard seed, ye might say unto this sycamine tree, Be thou plucked up by the root, and be thou planted in the sea; and it should obey you" (Luke 17:6).

Vocabulary Activities

1. suffer: Matthew 19:14

    a. Strong's Concordance (Greek): G863 αφιημι aphiemi, af-ee'-ay-mee

From G575 and ιημι hiemi (to send; an intensive form of ειμι eimi (to go)); to send forth, in various applications: - cry, forgive, forsake, lay aside, leave, **let (alone**, be, go, have), omit, put (send) away, remit, suffer, yield up.

    b. Webster's dictionary:

        1: a: to submit to or be forced to endure suffer martyrdom

            b: to feel keenly : labor under suffer thirst

        2: undergo, experience

        3: to put up with especially as inevitable or unavoidable

        4: **to allow** especially by reason of indifference the eagle suffers little birds to sing —William Shakespeare

Instruct the children to read Matthew 19:14 in their Bible. With their Bibles open, you can show them how to look up in a concordance (book or digital) the definition of a word, and then look at the word in a dictionary. Bring to their attention that one of the Hebrew definitions of suffer is to "let alone," or "let go." While Webster's dictionary is to "allow." This tells us that Jesus was saying to allow the children to come to Him and don't forbid them, or like the Hebrew definition, let them alone and allow the children to come to Jesus.

Follow this same process with the rest of the vocabulary words below. You may come up with more that you want to look up as a group.

2. humble: Matthew 18:4 G5013 ταπεινόω tapeinoo tap-i-no'-o

    a. From G5011; to depress; figuratively to humiliate (**in condition or heart**): -abase, bring low, humble (self).

    b. Webster:

        1: not proud or haughty; not arrogant or assertive

        2: reflecting, expressing, or offered **in a spirit of deference or submission** a humble apology

        3: a: ranking low in a hierarchy or scale; insignificant, unpretentious

            b: not costly or luxurious a humble contraption

Look up the rest of the definitions as a group. This will sharpen the skills of the Bible scholar on how to use a concordance and dictionary.

3. **sincere**: 1 Peter 2:2, 3

4. **handmaids**: Joel 2:28, 29; **Handmaidens:** Acts 2:17, 18

5. **courage**: Psalm 27:14

Definitions have been taken from:
1. Strong's Concordance in the e-Sword digital bible. https://1ref.us/1og (accessed March 30, 2021)
2. Webster's online dictionary. https://1ref.us/1oh (accessed March 30, 2021)

Writing a Short Essay

Topic Ideas

1. Favorite character in the Bible and why.
2. Ways the Lord can use children.
3. Strengths you have and how they can be used for Jesus.

Using one of the topics above you can also talk about how your favorite Bible character grabbed hold of Jehovah's strength, how you can grab hold of His strength, or how the Lord has strengthened you in the following ways.

Ways we can grab hold of the strength of the Lord.

1. Prayer (James 1:5)
2. Reading our Bible (Prov. 2:3–6; John 15:7)
3. Seeking advice from a godly person, then evaluating that advice by the Bible (Prov. 11:14)
4. Singing (Ps. 59:16, 17)
5. Joy (Neh. 8:10)
6. Obedience (Deut. 11:8; Ps. 103:20)
7. Trust (Isa. 30:15)

Explain to the children the basic writing format: introduction, subject/topic, and conclusion. Have them start their paper with the topic of interest. For this example, I will use the topic, "My favorite character in the Bible and why." In this example the essay will have five paragraphs, three of which will be my subject.

I. **Introduction** (The intro will overview the entire paper and tell the reader what you are going to say.)

II. **Subject** (Within each subject paragraph, the student should have a topic sentence and a conclusion sentence to tie the thoughts together.)

III. **Subject**

IV. **Subject**

V. **Conclusion** (Overview/summarizing the paper again, telling them what you already said by touching on the three topic/subject paragraphs.)

Sample Essay

For older children or more advanced writers, you can have them fill out an outline. You can also encourage them to have a topic sentence and a conclusion sentence for each of the subjects' paragraphs.

Topic: My favorite Bible character and why.

(I'm picking a character that the children may not pick, so they don't feel like they can't pick the character because it was the example.)

I. **Intro:** Nehemiah

II. **Subject/the why:** Love for his Maker and his country

    1. Wept, mourned, fasted, prayed: Neh. 1:4

    2. Confessed his sins and the sins of his people: Neh. 1:6–8

    3. Proclaimed promises of God: Neh. 1:8–11

III. **Subject/the why:** Brave: Neh. 2:1–12

    1. Makes request of king

    2. Grabs hold of power of God by prayer

    3. Steps forward by faith with continued requests (letters, timber)

IV. **Subject/the why:** Leader and Hard Worker

    1. Motivates people to rebuild wall vs. their homes: Neh. 2:17, 18

    2. Meets opposition with prayer: Neh. 4:9

    3. Labors with one hand ready to defend with other: Neh. 4:15

    4. Didn't even take off clothes but to wash/constantly ready

V. **Conclusion:** restate intro but in different words and reinforce main points

Once the overall outline is completed, go back and fill in the numbers for each subject, so the students will have ideas written down on the specific details they will be discussing. See sample outline on **page 23**.

Sample Outline

I. Intro/Topic _____

II. Subject _____

    1.

    2.

    3.

III. Subject _____

    1.

    2.

    3.

IV. Subject _____

    1.

    2.

    3.

V. Conclusion _____

Answer Key for Lesson 1

Learn How the Lord Will Prepare You for a Great Work (**p. 15**)

1. 1 John 5:4 — For whatsoever is **born** **of** **God** overcometh the world: and this is the **victory** that overcometh the world, *even* our **faith**.

2. 1 John 5:5 — Who is he that overcometh the world, but he that **believeth** that **Jesus** is the **Son** of **God**?

3. Luke 17:6 — And the Lord said, If ye had **faith** as a grain of **mustard** **seed**, ye might say unto this sycamine tree, Be thou **plucked** up by the root, and be thou planted in the **sea**; and it should obey you.

4. 1 John 5:14 — And this is the **confidence** that we have in him, that, if we ask any thing **according** to his **will**, he heareth us:

5. Romans 10:17 — So then **faith** *cometh* by **hearing**, and **hearing** by the **word** of God.

Get to Know Great Young People of the Bible (**p. 16**)

1. d
2. f
3. g
4. h
5. b
6. a
7. e
8. c

Angel of the Lord

Lesson 2

Prayer: Pray before each activity. Ask the Father for His Spirit to guide the minds of the students to learn more about Him and their Savior, Jesus Christ.

Activity 1

Different Names

Items Needed: 3x5 cards or small pieces of paper, tape

Have children write the different names they have on a piece of paper. Each name would go on a separate piece of paper. Names would include first, last, and middle names. Also, include nicknames that parents or friends might call them, shortened versions of their names. For older children you can talk about social security numbers being assigned to each name, and although they don't want to write down their number, they can put down the letters "SSN" to signify that this is another method in which people identify other people. We have employee numbers, membership numbers, phone numbers, all of which help to identify us. Once each name or identifying marker is written down on a separate sheet of paper, then have the class tape each piece of paper to their body. This will help children see a visual of how many names are associated with them. This will help them understand the concept that the same is true for Christ.

Discuss how that some places in Scripture an angel is a name to describe Jesus, just as we have many names. You can also discuss that there may be two people in the room whose name is Emily, but that doesn't mean they are the same person. There are many places in the Bible where the same name of an angel may be describing our Lord, and in others it may be describing a created angel. We must read around the verses for context. Reading around the verses is like looking at the characteristics of the two girls named Emily to see which one is which.

Explain that our Lord is so big and mighty, that He has so many ways to help us understand who He is, that we wouldn't be able to count how many names our Creator has. God has given us a few to help us to get to know Him a little better now, but we will spend all eternity getting to know Him more.

Activity 2

Darkness and Fear

Ask if there is anyone afraid of the dark. Older kids will probably say no, but in actuality if they were in a really dark place alone there would probably be some increase of the heart rate. Take the children into a very dark room where not a pinpoint of light is. Tell them not to say a word, everyone has to be quiet. For some this will be very uncomfortable. After several minutes of quiet, ask if anyone is uncomfortable about being in the dark room. Ask them if they are feeling better with the sound of your voice. If some say yes ask, "Why?" Some may say it is because they don't feel alone in the dark. Now take a small pin light out and turn it on. It should be a very small beam of light and tell the children to again sit very quietly and don't say a word. Let a couple minutes go by and ask them how they felt this time. Many will probably say it wasn't as bad as the first time. Ask them if they focused on the light. Ask them why they thought that little light made a difference? Leave the dark room and discuss with the students how Christ is the Light of the world (John 9:5). That the Word is also Light (Ps. 119:105). That Jesus is the Word (John 1:1, 14; Rev. 19:11–13; 1:5).

Discuss with the children that if we are afraid, and the darkness of this world is all around us, we need to focus on the Light, and that light is Christ. Focusing on Christ means focusing on His Word. Read the Word daily and hide it in your heart by memorizing it, so that you will have Light.

Activity 3

Nature Walk

Take the children on a walk to a place where you can see a variety of things in nature. Discuss how the Lord uses some of the things in nature to help us understand who He is. The following are some examples of items you might see.

Branch: Zechariah 3:8; 6:12; Isaiah 11:1; 53:2 (Christ grew out of the tribe of David.)

Vine: John 15:1–4 (The vine gives food to the shoots coming off of it; so does Christ give us the food we need through His Word.)

Rock: 1 Samuel 2:2; Psalm 95:1; 1 Corinthians 10:4 (The Lord is our strength.)

Sun: Revelation 22:16; 2 Peter 1:19; Luke 1:78; Numbers 24:17 (Jesus is brighter than the morning star/sun. When we see the sun with its life-giving rays, we should think of the life Christ gave to us through His death.)

Seed (word/Christ): seed = word: Luke 8:11 and word = Christ: John 1:1, 14; Revelation 1:5; 19:11–13 (Jesus lives within us when we read the Word and it grows in our heart like a seed planted in good soil.)

Lamb: John 1:29 (Jesus is the sacrificial Lamb so that we can be forgiven of our sins.)

Cow: Hebrews 9:12–14 (Heifers/cows were killed in the sanctuary, foreshadowing the death of Jesus.)

Rain/water: John 4:10–14 (Christ's Spirit is like living water to our soul.)

Snow: Psalm 51:7; Isaiah 1:18 (Our sin is like filthy rags, but the Lord wants to make us clean and bright like fresh snow.)

Flowers: Song of Solomon 2:1, 2 (rose or lily)

Gate/door: John 10:7, 9 (Jesus is the door to eternal life.)

Explain to the children that each one of the items discussed show us more about our Savior. These are like symbols for our Lord. Our God is so big, not one symbol can reveal who He is. It takes many symbols to help us get a picture of our Maker. Just as each child may have many names, and each one tells a little bit about who they are, so it is with our Lord and the many symbols discussed.

These symbols are created items. Just because the symbols are created doesn't mean Jesus was created. Christ is the One who created all things. He uses items that are familiar to us to show who He is. So it is with the symbol of an angel. It is a created being, but the Lord uses that symbol to reveal other aspects of who He is.

Word Scramble

Other Names or Symbols for Jesus

1. noLi (Hosea 11:10) _____

2. Lbma (John 1:29) _____

3. Rkco (1 Corinthians 10:4) _____

4. htiLg (John 8:12) _____

5. lAnge (Exodus 3:2–6, 14; John 8:58) _____

6. eotPphr (Mark 6:4) _____

7. rtsiPe (Hebrews 3:1) _____

8. nigK (Revelation 17:14) _____

9. ssrMgenee (Haggai 1:13; John 17:6–8) _____

10. haTcere (John 3:2) _____

11. etaorrC (Colossians 1:16) _____

12. Mhcalie (Daniel 10:21) _____

13. ahrlgAcne (Jude 1:9) _____

14. oavSriu (Luke 2:11) _____

Define

In Genesis 22:11 an angel is talking to Abraham. According to the Strong's Concordance, the Hebrew definition for the word angel in that text is: H4397 מַלְאָךְ, mal'âk mal-awk'

From an unused root meaning to despatch as a deputy; a messenger; specifically of God, that is, an angel (also a prophet, priest or teacher): — ambassador, angel, king, messenger.

Read the texts below and write in the blank the role Christ played in each text. **Clue:** look at the definition above and see if one of those roles defines what Christ is doing in the text.

1. John 17: 6, 8 _____

2. Mark 6:4 _____

3. John 3:2 _____

4. Hebrews 3:1 _____

5. Revelation 17:14 _____

Explain how knowing the characteristic of Christ in each answer above can help your walk in trusting in the Lord or becoming a better Christian.

1.

2.

3.

4.

5.

"And the angel of the LORD appeared unto him in a flame of fire out of the midst of a bush: and he looked, and, behold, the bush burned with fire, and the bush was not consumed. Moreover he said, I am the God of thy father, the God of Abraham, the God of Isaac, and the God of Jacob. And Moses hid his face; for he was afraid to look upon God" (Exod. 3:2, 6).

Angel of the Lord | 31

Bookmark

An angel is just another symbol to help us understand the different phases of Christ's ministry. Searching out all the symbols that represent Christ helps us to realize that He is our all in all. Your role may change as you get older, but you are still you. It is the same with Jesus. He is constantly working to save us and each symbol helps us to understand that a little better.

Print pages 31 and 32, double sided, in order to have front and back to the bookmarks. Cut the bookmark out.

Note: Use cardstock paper or laminate it if using thinner paper.

"And there was war in heaven: Michael and his angels fought against the dragon; and the dragon fought and his angels, and prevailed not; neither was their place found any more in heaven. And the great dragon was cast out, that old serpent, called the Devil, and Satan, which deceiveth the whole world: he was cast out into the earth, and his angels were cast out with him. And I heard a loud voice saying in heaven, Now is come salvation, and strength, and the kingdom of our God, and the power of his Christ: for the accuser of our brethren is cast down, which accused them before our God day and night" (Rev. 12:7–10).

Answer Key for Lesson 2

Word Scramble (p. 28)

1. Lion
2. Lamb
3. Rock
4. Light
5. Angel
6. Prophet
7. Priest
8. King
9. Messenger
10. Teacher
11. Creator
12. Michael
13. Archangel
14. Saviour (American English uses Savior while all other English uses Saviour—great conversation to have with the children about the differences.)

Define (p. 29)

1. John 17:6, 8— Messenger
2. Mark 6:4— Prophet
3. John 3:2— Teacher
4. Hebrews 3:1— High Priest
5. Revelation 17:14— King

The Covenant

Lesson 3

Prayer: Pray before each activity. Ask the Father for His Spirit to guide the minds of the students to learn more about Him and their Savior, Jesus Christ.

Activity 1

Refracting Light

Items needed: flashlight or other light source and a prism

Discuss with the children that light refraction is where light travels from one medium and then goes through another medium with a different density. This can cause a bending of the light that can separate it into its color components.

Example: Take your light source and shine it. The light is moving through the air. Your other medium or substance is the prism. The light travels through the air then through the prism. This will cause the light to bend and break the white light into the colors of a rainbow.

Notice how Jesus is called the Light of the world (John 8:12). Light can be broken down into a rainbow. If Jesus is Light, and a rainbow is just light separated, then a rainbow must also be a symbol for Jesus, which is just another colorful way of showing the different characteristics of Christ.

Activity 2

Color Wheel

Items needed: crayons, heavy cardstock paper, and fishing line (10 inches per student) or tough string

Explain to the children how we are learning about symbols of Jesus. Each symbol is like a color that gives us a little more information about who our Lord is. The rainbow is another one of those symbols. The rainbow is made up of many colors but when combined it creates white light. Jesus is the light.

Make a color wheel and see how each color blends together to make white.

1. Print color wheel on heavy card stock paper.

2. Color your wheel (on both sides) with the colors of the rainbow using the acronym ROY G BIV (red, orange, yellow, green, blue, indigo, violet). Students will just use violet for both violet and indigo.

3. Cut color wheel out.

4. Poke a hole in the center of color wheel and thread your fishing line through.

5. With one hand on one end of the line and the other hand at the other end spin the color wheel which will be in the middle. If spun fast enough all the colors will disappear and the paper will appear white.

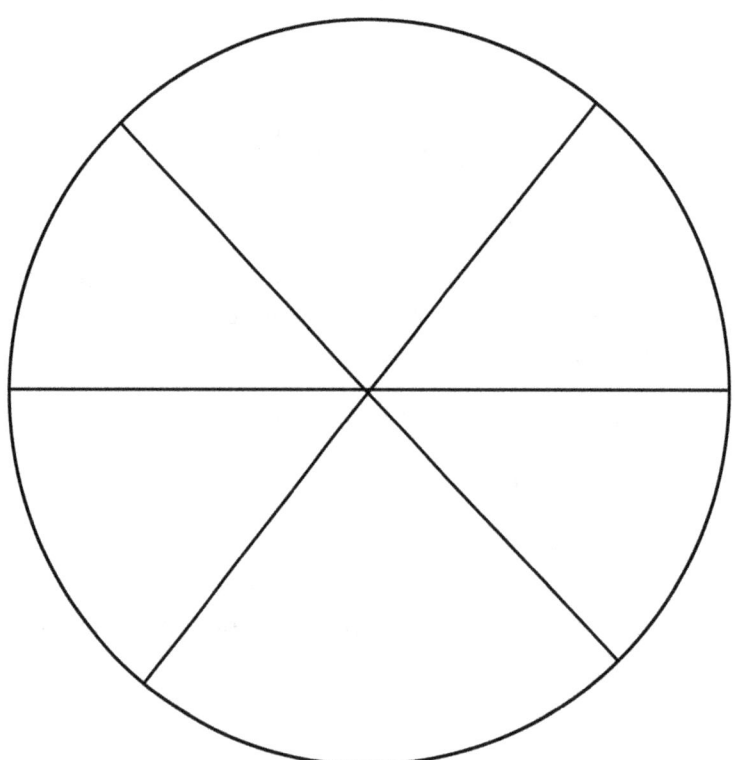

Practicing Dictionary Use

Look up the following words in a dictionary and write the definition in the space provided.

1. Covenant:

2. Promise:

3. Oath:

4. Pledge:

5. Vow:

6. Bond:

7. Synonym:

How important is it for you to keep your word?

How important is it for others to keep their vow to you?

Word Scramble

A Promise through Clothes

1. What were the first clothes man was given? Psalm 104:2

   (lgith) _____

2. What was the second pair of clothes man had? Genesis 3:6, 7

   (vlaees) _____

3. What was Adam and Eve's third pair of clothes? Genesis 3:21; Revelation 13:8

   (mbal nsksi) _____

4. What clothing does the Lord want to put on us today? Psalm 37:6

   (tsshienrseogu) _____

5. What clothes did Christ put on in order to save us? 1 Peter 4:1

   (mnuah shefl) _____

Do our clothes show that we have faith in Jesus?

Multiple Choice

The Covenant

Circle the correct answer.

1. **What Promise did Jesus make to Adam and Eve?**
    A. They would never have to leave the garden.
    B. Satan would not tempt them.
    C. Jesus would come to earth as a baby (seed of the woman).
    D. There would be no pain.

2. **Did Jesus keep His word to Adam and Eve?**
    A. Yes
    B. No

3. **What is one covenant Jesus gave to us?**
    A. We would never have any problems.
    B. He would forgive us of our sins.
    C. I can have anything I want.

4. **If Jesus kept His promise to Adam and Eve, do you think that He will keep His oath to us?**
    A. Yes
    B. No

5. **When the devil says you are a sinner and will never be good enough to go to heaven because your sin is too great, what should you do?**
    A. Believe him.
    B. Ask for forgiveness for your sins.
    C. Work harder so the Lord will forgive you.
    D. Believe that Jesus died for your sins and will forgive you of your sins.
    E. Both B and D.

6. **Why can we be forgiven of our sins?**
    A. Because I asked.
    B. Because the Father loves us.

C. Because Jesus took our punishment on the cross.

D. All of the above.

7. We must have faith to believe that Jesus loves us and that He will forgive us of our sins if we ask.

    A. True

    B. False

8. The covenant of Christ was only given at the foundation of the world.

    A. True

    B. False

9. The following are examples of the promise that Christ would come as our Savior and die on the cross.

    A. The seed of the woman would crush Satan.

    B. A fig tree would wither.

    C. Abraham would be the father of many nations.

    D. The Passover lamb was killed and blood put on the door posts.

    E. A rainbow was given at the flood.

    F. All except B.

10. What is one promise that we are waiting to have fulfilled?

    A. No more pain or sorrow.

    B. Earth made new.

    C. Jesus coming again.

    D. All of the above.

11. If Jesus kept all of His other promises, can we trust He will keep the promise to come again?

    A. True

    B. False

12. Would you like to have Jesus as your Lord and Savior?

    A. Yes

    B. No

Answer Key for Lesson 3

A Promise through Clothes (p. 38)

1. light
2. leaves
3. lamb skins
4. righteousness
5. human flesh

How can the way we dress today show that we have faith in Jesus? As Christians we should be living a lifestyle that glorifies our Savior. The way we dress and act does not save us, but Jesus said, "By their fruits you shall know them." By the way we dress and act will reveal to others that we love Jesus. The goal is to lead others to Christ. If we dress immodestly or wear clothes with characters that do not glorify our Savior, this might be an indicator that our faith in Him might be lacking. Only you can evaluate yourself, go before the Lord, and ask Jesus if you are walking according to His will for your life.

Multiple Choice—The Covenant (p. 39)

1. C
2. A
3. B
4. A
5. E
6. D
7. A
8. B
9. F

Testament

Lesson 4

Prayer: Pray before each activity. Ask the Father for His Spirit to guide the minds of the students to learn more about Him and their Savior, Jesus Christ.

Activity 1

Built on the Rock

Items Needed: Rocky area

Go somewhere outside where there are plenty of rocks. Ask the children to see how tall of a structure they can build with the rocks. This can be done individually or in teams if you have lots of children. Give them about 15 minutes. When finished compare the different structures. Ask the children to analyze which ones are the biggest and why they thought the builders were able to build them so high. Find out what could be done differently next time for those who couldn't get theirs as high.

Some tips could be that the base or foundation was not big enough. Look at the ground; if it is uneven then it would make the structure wobbly. You don't put small rocks on the bottom, but you put big rocks for a better foundation.

Explain to children how knowing the different aspects of Christ helps us to build a better understanding of who He is. Jesus is the rock, and each synonym for Him is a rock of truth which helps us know our Savior better.

Activity 2

Red Rover

Items Needed: Outdoors, at least ten children

Have children split up into two teams. Have teams about ten yards apart in a line facing each other. Children will be holding hands. Team A will decide who they will call from the other team to run over and try to break through the chain. If child from Team B breaks through then they get to pick someone from Team A to go with them back to Team B. If child from Team B does not break through then they stay on Team A's side. Team B now decides who they want to call over to their side. Child from Team A runs to team B trying to break through. If they do then they pick someone from Team B to go back to Team A. If they don't then they stay on Team B's side. This game goes back and forth until one person is left on one side or until timer stops for game to be ended.

Explain to the children that each child represents truth. When the chain is broken the team is separated and it is not as strong. It is the same with God's word. When we don't know the chain of truth then our understanding of who Jesus is, is not as strong.

Coded Words Puzzle

Use the following code to uncover the coded terms in the sentences below.

A	B	C	D	E	F	G	H	I	J	K	L	M
1	2	3	4	5	6	7	8	9	10	11	12	13
N	O	P	Q	R	S	T	U	V	W	X	Y	Z
14	15	16	17	18	19	20	21	22	23	24	25	26

__ __ __ __ __ __ __ __ __ __
9 14 20 8 5 2 9 2 12 5

__ __ __ __ __ __ __ __ ,
20 5 19 20 1 13 5 14 20

__ __ __ __ __ __ __ __ , __ __ __
3 15 22 5 14 1 14 20 1 14 4

__ __ __ __ __ __ __ __ __ __ __ __
20 5 19 20 9 13 15 14 25 1 18 5

__ __ __ __ __ __ __ __ __ __
19 25 14 15 14 25 13 19 6 15 18

__ __ __ __ __ __ __ __ __ .
5 1 3 8 15 20 8 5 18

Acts of the Promise

Jesus made a promise that He would come and pay our price on the cross. He also promised that He would come again. He gave actions for the Hebrews to remind them of the promise. Some of those were sacrificing animals to point to Him. Others included going to Jerusalem during the Passover and celebrating the feasts. These were promises in action to remind the people of the Promise of God to send His Son to die for us, and that He would return again.

1. Are there actions that you do today that remind you of Jesus' promises?

2. According to your answer for number one, how does that action remind you of the promise or promises of God?

3. How might that action be turned into an action where someone might forget the promises?

Answer Key for Lesson 4

Coded Word Puzzle (p. 44)

In the Bible, "testament," "covenant," and "testimony" are synonyms for each other.

Acts of Promise (p. 45)

1. Common actions that can remind us of Jesus' promises: praying, going to church, listening to Christian music, reading our Bibles.

2. Answers vary.

3. When we put faith in the action itself, and forget about who it points to. When we think the action makes us better, instead of realizing that only the One it points to (Christ) makes us better.

The Law

Lesson 5

Prayer: Pray before each activity. Ask the Father for His Spirit to guide the minds of the students to learn more about Him and their Savior, Jesus Christ.

Activity 1

Law of Gravity

Items Needed: A book and a pencil or pen; a large heavy ball and a smaller lighter ball

Tell the children that you will need a volunteer to drop the book and pencil at the same time. But before the volunteer comes up, ask: **which item they think will hit the ground first**? Note the answers.

- Have volunteer come up and drop the book and pen at the same time. Next have another volunteer drop the two balls at the same time. You can also use other items you have lying around to allow all the children a chance to experiment.

Ask—

1. **Why did the items drop?** *Answer*: law of gravity

2. **What is the law of gravity?** *Answer*: Every particle attracts every other particle in the universe with a force that is equal to the product of their masses and inversely proportional to the square of the distance between their centers.[1] Isaac Newton's formula: $F = G \frac{m_1 m_2}{r^2}$

3. **What is a law?** *Answer*: A law is a constant, observable phenomenon.

4. **Why did the items hit the ground at the same time?** *Answer*: Newton's Law of Acceleration. Newton's second law states that the acceleration of an object is directly related to the net force, and inversely related to its mass.[2] For instance the larger object has more mass, or you can say it weighs more, so it takes longer for the object to accelerate because of the resistance of its weight/mass.

---
1 https://1ref.us/1oi (accessed March 30, 2021)
2 https://1ref.us/1oj (accessed March 30, 2021)

5. **Some people say airplanes defy the law of gravity. What do you think? Is gravity still present?** *Answer*: Yes, gravity is still present even though an airplane can fly.

6. **How does an airplane work?** *Answer*: The engine of the plane pushes the plane forward while the angle of the wing drives the speeding air downward. Therefore, the force on the bottom of the wing is higher than the force on the top of the wing, thus driving the airplane up.[3] Remember Newton's law about force?

Spiritual Application

God's law, the Ten Commandments, is binding, even though some think they can defy God's law. Yet, like an airplane, we have been promised that we can fly. "But they that wait upon the LORD shall renew their strength; they shall mount up with wings as eagles; they shall run, and not be weary; and they shall walk, and not faint" (Isa. 40:31).

Think of us as airplanes and the Ten Commandments as the law of gravity. The law is still there, even though the plane can fly. Sin is that force upon us that keeps us down, while Christ is the engine pushing us forward, decreasing the force or weight upon us, to propel us upward to Him (Matt. 11:28, 29). Even though Christ paid the price for sin, the law is still present; it is still binding. Every time we sin it forces us down, while every time we reach out to Jesus, the force pushing down on us diminishes (Prov. 24:16). When we seek Christ, the desire to sin will eventually lessen, therefore lessening the force on us. This doesn't happen overnight, but waiting on the Lord and renewing your strength in Him will result in flying (Isa. 40:31).

Note to teacher: It might be advantageous to talk to the child that this concept is dealing with victories, not salvation. Salvation is free, while exercising our spiritual muscles in victory is like any process of growth (Luke 13:6–9).

---

3 https://1ref.us/1ok (accessed March 30, 2021)

Basic Meaning of the Law

Answer the following in a complete sentence.

1. If you break the law by speeding, what will happen to you?

2. If the police officer doesn't give you a ticket, it is called what?

3. If there were no speeding laws, would you be breaking the law if you were speeding?

4. What is sin? (1 John 3:4)

5. If you break the law of God, what is the sentence? (Rom. 6:23)

6. If there was no law, would there be sin? (Rom. 5:13)

7. Because Jesus died on the cross and took our punishment for sin, does that mean that the law is no longer binding? (Rom. 3:28, 31)

Synonyms

Look-up the texts and write the synonyms for each section.

	Synonyms for Christ			Synonyms for Commandments
John 1:14	1.			1.
Hebrews 12:24	2.	Exodus 34:28		2.
Galatians 3:17	3.	Exodus 24:12		3.
Matthew 26:28	4.			4.
Ephesians 2:20	5.	Exodus 31:18		5.

Do you see how all the words that are used for the law are also used for Jesus? This is why David said that the law of God is exceedingly broad. When David looked at the Law, he saw Christ and said, "I have seen the end of all perfection" (Ps. 119:96). He saw Christ's perfect life for our sinful one.

1. Does Jesus change? (Mal. 3:6; Heb. 13:8)

2. If the law is another representation of Jesus, then does the law change? (Gal. 3:15, 17)

3. Look up "disannul" in the dictionary and write the definition.

4. Write the definition of "annul."

5. Write the synonym for "disannul/annul" in the blank below.

   "And this I say, *that* the covenant, that was confirmed before of God in Christ, the law, which was four hundred and thirty years after, cannot _____, that it should make the promise of none effect" (Gal. 3:17).

6. The moral law is a symbol for Christ. It is a covenant or promise of His life and His character. Do you think Christ is going to change or make void one portion of that law, for example, the fourth commandment?

Breaking down the Text

"For the law maketh men high priests which have infirmity; but the word of the oath, which was since the law, *maketh* the Son, who is consecrated for evermore" (Heb. 7:28).

1. Circle the word in the text above that was supplied and was not in the original Greek.

2. Look up the word "maketh" in a concordance and write its meaning.

3. Fill in the blank with the synonym for maketh.

    For the law _____ men high priests which have infirmity.

4. Write some other synonyms for oath. If you don't remember look back in your lesson.

5. Write one of the synonyms for oath in the blank below.

    …. but the word of the _____, which was since the law.

6. Now let's combine the blanks. Fill in the synonyms for what you have already done.
    For the law _____ men high priests which have infirmity, but the word of the _____, which was since the law.

7. In your own words describe what the text is saying in number 6.

8. Now fill in the blanks below and add another name for who the "Son" is. We will leave out the second "maketh" since it was supplied.

    For the law (synonym for maketh) _____ men high priests which have infirmity,

    but the word of the (synonym for oath)_____, which was since the law, the

    _____.

9. Write the definition of an appositive.

10. Write two sentences with an appositive.

11. Circle the appositive in the sentence below.

    "For the law maketh men high priests which have infirmity; but the word of the oath, which was since the law, *maketh* the Son, who is consecrated for evermore" (Heb. 7:28).

12. Son is a noun that is renaming what noun right next to it?

13. Look up the word "consecrated" in the concordance and write the definition.

14. Fill in the blanks below with the synonyms you have looked up.

    "For the law (synonym for maketh) _____ men high priests which have infirmity, but the word of the _____, which was since the law, the (synonym for oath) _____, who is (synonym for consecrated) _____ for evermore" (Heb. 7:28).

15. In your own words explain the entire text of Hebrews 7:28.

16. Fill in the blank with the synonym for the supplied *maketh*.

    "For the law <u>appointed</u> men high priests which have infirmity, but the word of the <u>covenant</u>, which was since the law, _____ the <u>Christ</u>, who is <u>perfect</u> for evermore" (Heb. 7:28).

17. If we left in the supplied *maketh*, would it change the meaning of the text?

The ceremonial law was a symbol of Christ in action. It pointed to His life without blemish or spot and then His death for us.

Character

Write down some characteristics of who you are. Don't use descriptive language for what you look like on the outside but what you look like on the inside. For example, are you kind? Are you patient? Do you tend to be helpful to others?

Now write down some characteristics of who you want to be, but maybe you haven't quite mastered those qualities. Some examples may be: you might want to be more loving to others. You might want to be a hard worker and more diligent in your tasks.

How do the Ten Commandments relate to Christ's character?

Answer Key for Lesson 5

Basic Meaning of the Law (p. 49)

Make sure children wrote in complete sentences. For space purposes, the answers below are not in complete sentences.

1. If you speed, what will happen to you? **pay the penalty, ticket**
2. If the police officer doesn't give you a ticket, it is called what? **mercy or grace**
3. If there were no speeding, laws would you be breaking the law if you were speeding? **no**
4. What is sin? (1 John 3:4) **transgression of the law**
5. If you break the law of God, what is the sentence? (Rom. 6:23) **death**
6. If there was no law, would there be sin? (Rom. 5:13) **NO**
7. Because Jesus died on the cross and took our punishment for sin, does that mean that the law is no longer binding? (Rom. 3:28, 31) **NO it does not; the law is binding**

Synonyms (p. 50)

	Synonyms for Christ		Synonyms for Commandments
John 1:14	1. Word	Exodus 34:28	1. word
Hebrews 12:24	2. Covenant	Exodus 24:12	2. covenant
Galatians 3:17	3. Law		3. law
Matthew 26:28	4. Testament	Exodus 31:18	4. testimony
Ephesians 2:20	5. Stone		5. stone

1. Does Jesus change? (Mal. 3:6; Heb. 13:8) **NO**
2. If the law is another representation of Jesus then does the law change? (Gal. 3:15,17) **NO, it cannot be disannulled**

3. Look up disannul in the dictionary and write the definition. **Annul or cancel,** https://1ref.us/1ol (accessed March 30, 2021)

4. Write the definition of annul. **Invalid or void,** https://1ref.us/1om (accessed March 30, 2021)

5. Write the synonym for disannul in the blank.

"And this I say, *that* the covenant, that was confirmed before of God in Christ, the law, which was four hundred and thirty years after, cannot <u>void</u>, that it should make the promise of none effect" (Gal. 3:17)

Breaking Down the Text (p. 51)

"For the law maketh men high priests which have infirmity; but the word of the oath, which was since the law, *maketh* the Son, who is consecrated for evermore" (Heb. 7:28)

1. Circle the word above that was supplied in the text and was not in the original Greek.

2. Look in the concordance what the word "maketh" means.

    G2525 καθίστημι kathistēmi kath-is'-tay-mee From G2596 and G2476; to place down (permanently), that is, (figuratively) **to designate**, constitute, convoy: - **appoint**, be, conduct, **make, ordain**, set.

3. Fill in the blank with the synonym for maketh.

    For the law **appointed** men high priests which have infirmity.

4. Write some other synonyms for oath. If you don't remember look back in your lesson.

Covenant or promise

5. Write one of the synonyms for oath in the blank below.

    …. but the word of the **covenant/promise,** which was since the law.

6. Now let's combine the blanks. Fill in the synonyms for what you have already done.

    For the law **appointed** men high priests which have infirmity, but the word of the **covenant**, which was since the law.

7. In your own words describe what the text is saying in number 6.

    According to the law sinful men were ordained to be high priests. But the covenant was at the time of the law.

8. Now fill in the blanks below and add another name for who the "Son" is. We will leave out the second "maketh" since it was supplied.

For the law <u>appointed</u> men high priests which have infirmity, but the word of the <u>covenant</u>, which was since the law, the <u>Christ/Jesus</u>.

9. Write the definition of an appositive.

   An appositive is a noun or noun phrase that renames another noun right beside it. https://1ref.us/1on (accessed March 30, 2021)

10. Write two sentences with an appositive.

    - John, the captain, sailed the ship across the ocean. ("the captain" is the appositive)
    - John, the tall captain, sailed the ship across the ocean. ("the tall captain" is the appositive)
    - During dinner, Ashur, the messiest two-year-old ever, spewed mashed potatoes like and erupting volcano. ("the messiest two-year-old ever" is the appositive)

11. Circle the appositive in the sentence below.

    "For the law maketh men high priests which have infirmity; but the word of the oath, which was since the law, *maketh* the (Son) who is consecrated for evermore" (Heb. 7:28).

12. Son is a noun that is renaming what noun right next to it?

    The Son (Jesus) is renaming the law, which is right next to it.

13. Look up the word consecrated in the concordance and write the definition.

    G5048 τελειόω teleioo tel-i-o'-o From G5046; to complete, that is, (literally) accomplish, or (figuratively) consummate (in character): - **consecrate, finish, fulfil, (make) perfect.**

14. Fill in the blanks below with the synonyms you have looked up.

    "For the law **appointed** men high priests which have infirmity, but the word of the **covenant**, which was since the law, the **Christ**, who is **perfect** for evermore" (Heb. 7:28). [Is this not referring to the law of the priesthood and not the 10 Commandments, since the commandments do not appoint priests?]

15. In your own words explain the entire text of Hebrews 7:28.

    According to the law sinful men were ordained to be high priests. But the covenant was at the time of the law, which is Christ who is perfect forever.

16. Fill in the blank with the synonym for the supplied *maketh*.

    "For the law <u>appointed</u> men high priests which have infirmity, but the word of the <u>covenant</u>, which was since the law, **<u>appointed</u>** the <u>Christ</u>, who is <u>perfect</u> for evermore" (Heb. 7:28).

17. If we left in the supplied *maketh* would it change the meaning of the text?

No, it would be saying, "According to the law sinful men were ordained to be high priests. But the covenant was at the time of the law, which is Christ who is perfect forever and fulfilled the law." Remember one of the definitions for consecrate is fulfill. So we could add the word fulfil in the blank as well.

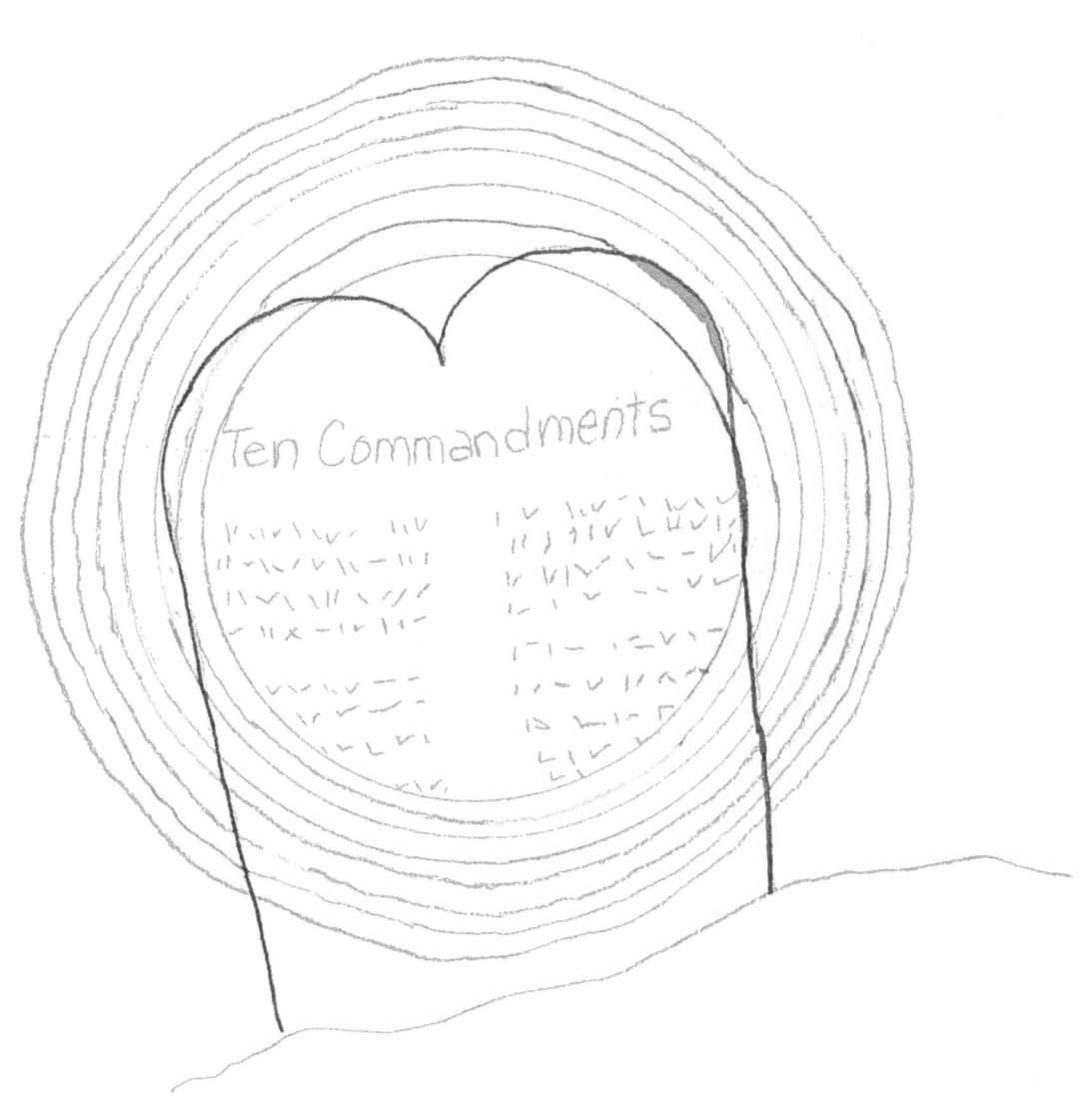

Prophecy

Lesson 6

Prayer: Pray before each activity. Ask the Father for His Spirit to guide the minds of the students to learn more about Him and their Savior, Jesus Christ.

Activity 1

Prophecy through Nature

Items needed: tree, river, rock (or a picture of them), Bibles

Go for a walk where you can see trees, rocks, and a river or some sort of water. Ask the children what a tree has to do with prophecy. Give children some time to think and come up with answers. Once you feel like enough time is given, have them look up Matthew 24:32. Have one of the children read the verse and then ask the question again.

—What does a tree have to do with prophecy? **Answer:** The Lord used a fig tree to illustrate a prophetic event, the end of the world/second coming.

As you walk a little further ask the children what a rock has to do with prophecy. Hopefully their mind is making more connections after the first example. Give them some time to think and answer then have them look up Daniel 2:44, 45. Have a child read the text then recap the story and ask the question again.

—What does a rock have to do with prophecy? **Answer:** The rock represents Christ and is used to illustrate the second coming.

Now ask the children what water has to do with prophecy? Follow the above format, having them read John 7:37–39.

—What does a river have to do with prophecy? **Answer:** A river was used as a symbol for the outpouring of the Holy Spirit.

Conclusion: If these items can be used as symbols to reveal future events and to reveal Christ, can you see how a promise/covenant, the gospel, or the law can represent future events associated with Christ?

Activity 2

Prophecy Revealing the Unseen

Items needed: chair, ball, balloons (balloon for each student), Bibles

Have a child stand on a chair with arms out. Instruct a couple of students to examine the area between the hands and the floor of the student who is on the chair. Note their responses. You may need to ask: **Do you see anything between (*name of child*)'s hands and the floor?** When the children say no, that they don't see anything between their hands and floor, tell them there is indeed something there. Letting them know that there is something there might help them think past the seen. Give them a chance to come up with gravity. If they can't come up with gravity, then tell them it is gravity between the arms and the floor. Ask them: **Can you see gravity?** *Answer:* No. *Question*: **How do you know it is there?** Let them answer and then give the student on the chair a ball to drop. *Explain*: **We can't see gravity but we can see the effects of gravity. Just like we can't see wind but we can see the effects of wind in the trees. Just because we can't see something doesn't mean it is not real.**

Blow air out of your mouth and ask the students if they saw anything come out? The answer is *no*, but ask them if something did come out. The answer is *yes*. Could they see the air? *No*. Does that mean it isn't there? *No*. Give everyone a balloon. Have them blow up their balloon and explain how the air is so powerful that it can expand the elastic balloon and allow it to get bigger. *Ask*: **Do we see the effects the air had on the balloon?** *Answer*: Yes. Now have the students let go of their balloon and let it fly around the room. *Ask*: **Did you see the effects of the air coming out of the balloon?** *Answer*: Yes. *Explain*: **So, we can't see gravity and we can't see air, but they are real, right? Because we can see their effects. The same is true about prophecy. Prophecy is the evidence of the unseen. When the prediction comes to pass it brings with it faith in the Lord. It helps us to realize that Jesus is Lord and His Word stands true.**

Have the children look up John 13:19.

"Now I tell you before it come, that, when it is come to pass, ye may believe that I am he" (John 13:19).

Prophecy helps us believe that Jesus is Lord. For some, prophecy may be hard to understand, but it is a very important piece in the puzzle in knowing our Savior. I pray that you will not get discouraged when trying to understand prophecy. Remember not to give up—you can do and learn hard things with Christ.

Name _____

Complete the crossword puzzle below.

Across

4. Prophecy helps us _____. (John 14:29)
5. When the Bible makes a promise it is call a _____, which is also a prophecy of the future event.
6. A prediction of the future is called _____.
8. One symbol for prophecy is _____. (Revelation 19:10)
10. Prophecy is supposed to reveal who? (John 13:19)
11. Christ is the _____ of time because He will be our light and there will be no more darkness. (Revelation 22:5)
14. What started time at the beginning of creation? (Genesis 1:1–5)
15. A blessing is given to those who _____ prophecy.

Down

1. A prophecy given with a duration of time is called a _____ prophecy.
2. Jesus linked Himself with time when He said He was the Alpha and _____. (Revelation 22:13)
3. Jesus' blood is called the _____ which is a prophecy of His death. (Hebrews 9:18–22)
7. Prophecy is a _____ letter to us from our Lord.
9. A prophecy based on a specific scenario is called an _____ prophecy.
12. The combination of light and _____ results in a day or time. (Genesis 1:1–5)
13. The Bible says that the _____ prophesied. (Matthew 11:13)

Prophecy Short Answer

In complete sentences answer the following questions.

1. What are the two types of prophecy?

2. Look up in a concordance what the Greek definition for "testimony" is in Revelation 19:10.

3. As it relates to Jesus, why is prophecy important? (John 13:19) Use one of the words from the definition in question two for your answer.

4. Give an example of how prophecy can also be a covenant.

5. Give an example of how the testament can also be a prophecy. (Isa. 53:5–7; Matt. 26:28; Heb. 9:18–20)

6. Give an example of how the law is a prophecy. (John 1:45; Luke 24:44; Matt. 11:13)

Answer Key for Lesson 6

Crossword Puzzle (p. 60)

<u>Across</u>

    4. Believe

    5. covenant

    6. prophecy

    8. testimony

    10. Jesus

    11. end

    14. light

    15. read

<u>Down</u>

    1. time

    2. Omega

    3. testimony

    7. love

    9. event

    12. dark

    13. law

Prophecy Short Answer (p. 63)

1. The two types of prophecy are time prophecy and event prophecy.

2. Strong's Concordance: G3141 μαρτυρία marturia mar-too-ree'-ah From G3144; evidence given (judicially or generally): - record, report, testimony, witness.

3. Prophecy gives evidence that Jesus is the Great I Am.

4. Answers may vary. If students write any promise given by the Lord or a prophet where the promise was fulfilled then this would be a covenant/promise as well as a prophecy.

5. Answers may vary: Christ is called the testament (Hebrews 7:22) and it was the prediction that Christ would come and die on the cross for our sins which was a testament or covenant give to the Hebrews in action.

6. Answers may vary. The law prophesied of Christ's sinless life.

Meat

Lesson 7

Prayer: Pray before each activity. Ask the Father for His Spirit to guide the minds of the students to learn more about Him and their Savior, Jesus Christ.

Activity 1

All Have Sinned

Items Needed: Masking tape, corn starch, broom, one six-foot 2x4 piece of lumber, one three-foot 2x4 piece of lumber, one hammer, and 3–4 nails (at least 3" long nails)

Part A

You will want to perform this activity outside on concrete, in a gym, or in a kitchen. It will be a bit messy. Using the masking tape, make a square large enough for someone to stand in (about 18 inches square). Using the masking tape, make a separate rectangle (path) from the 18-inch square. Make sure the rectangle isn't longer than six feet. See below for the set-up, black lines represent masking tape.

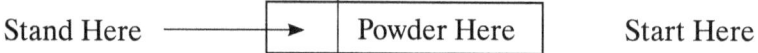

Once you have the area taped off sprinkle a thick layer of corn starch in the long rectangular path. Then explain to the children that, with bare feet, they are to walk down the path of the powder and step into the clean box at the end, trying to not get powder in the box. Give each child a turn sweeping the box out after each child to see how each student did. When each child has had a turn have them look up the following texts.

Romans 3:23: How many have sinned?

Isaiah 64:6: What does our sin look like to God?

Romans 6:23: What should be our punishment?

The powder is like sin—it is messy and filthy. Just as our feet became messy with powder, each one of our lives is filthy with sin.

Read Exodus 33:18–23. **Why couldn't Moses see the face of the Father?** *Answer*: Because Moses had sin on him like the powder. God is so holy and clean that there is not even a speck of sin anywhere on Him. Moses could not look at His face and live while he still had sin on him.

Part B

Now take the children to an area that has been set up with the wood, nails, and hammer. Tell them that we are going to build a cross. Ask for one or two volunteers to take turns hammering the three-foot 2x4 onto the six-foot 2x4 to make a cross. As the students are doing this, talk about how Christ must have felt being nailed to the cross: how painful it was, how sad He must have been because the people He loved were hurting Him.

Have a volunteer read:

- Matthew 27:27–36: **Let's pause for a moment to ponder how Jesus must have felt**.

- Ephesians 1:3–7: **What has Christ done for us?** *Answer*: Because Christ died for us, we have been adopted into the family of God. This was the plan from the beginning, that Christ would bridge the gap between us and the Father because of sin.

Take the cross over to the powder area and use the cross as a bridge across the path of sin. Have the students walk along the 4-inch section of the lumber to get to the "clean" area without getting powder (sin) on them. Allow each student a turn to walk across the bridge.

Have a volunteer read:

- 1 Corinthians 2:2: **What did Paul say was the only thing he wanted to know?** *Answer*: 1. Christ 2. the crucifixion.

- 2 Peter 3:18: **Who are we commanded to know?** *Answer*: Jesus

Ask the students:

1. If we are called to know Christ Jesus, then do we want to know all of Him?

2. Do you think we should pick and choose what aspects we want to know about Him?

3. Christ is the meat of the Bible, and there are aspects about knowing Him that might be a little harder to understand, like prophecy. Just because some aspects about Christ might be harder to understand, do you think we should give up on those, like prophecy?

4. Being willing to search the deeper aspects of Christ is eating the meat of the Word of God. Do you think this is important? After all, He is the one that bridges the gap between us and the Father. If you were to cross a bridge, wouldn't you want to know everything about it to make sure it is safe?

The Bible Explains Itself

Look up the following texts and write down how God's word uses the word *meat*.

<u>Literal Applications</u>

1. Genesis 1:29: _____ and _____

2. Leviticus 2:4: _____ or _____

3. Ezekiel 16:19 _____, _____, and _____

4. Luke 24:30 _____

5. Acts 2:46 _____

<u>Spiritual Applications</u>

6. Hebrews 5:12, 13 _____

7. John 4:34 _____

8. John 6:55, 63 _____ or His _____

Meat in Action

Answer the questions below in complete sentences.

1. What are three spiritual applications of meat? (John 4:34; Hebrews 5:12, 13; John 6:55, 63)

2. Read the following verses and state who was performing the meat of the Lord and who was not (Luke 10:25–37). State exactly what meat was being performed in this text.

3. Is there hope for those who do not perform the meat (obey) of the Lord? (Luke 15:11–32). What did the individual have to do in the story?

4. Give some examples on how you might (obey) perform the meat of the Lord. Give some examples of where you haven't (obeyed) performed the meat of the Lord and how you can have hope during those times.

Writing a Short Essay

Have the children write a short essay explaining how meat is a symbol for Jesus and how it is also a symbol for the deep truths of God for example prophecy. Here are some Bible verses to give them to guide them in their thoughts.

Hebrews 5:12, 13; Hebrews 6:5; John 4:34; John 6:55, 63; Psalm 119:103; 1 Timothy 4:6, 14; 1 Corinthians 12:31; 14:1, 39; 2 Peter 1:17–19

Here is a sample outline that you can share with the students, or you may want to come up with one, as a class or one-on-one with the children.

Example 1

- I   **Intro:** The message of Christ is meat.
- II   **Subject:** Christ is the Word.
- III   **Subject:** Christ's words are meat.
- IV   **Subject:** Prophecy is meat.
- V   **Conclusion:** Don't neglect Christ, which means we don't want to neglect prophecy.

Example 2

- I   **Intro:** Meat
- II   **Subject:** Milk vs. Meat
- III   **Subject:** Who/what is spiritual meat?
- IV   **Subject:** Know Christ by this knowledge
- V   **Conclusion:** Application

Sample Outline

I. Intro/Topic _____

II. Subject _____

    1.

    2.

    3.

III. Subject _____

    1.

    2.

    3.

IV. Subject _____

    1.

    2.

    3.

V. Conclusion _____

Answer Key for Lesson 7

The Bible Explains Itself (p. 68)

1. herbs and fruit
2. cake or wafer
3. flour, oil, and honey
4. a meal
5. bread
6. skillful in the word/understanding deep truths of the Word
7. doing the will of the Father/obedience
8. Jesus or His words

Meat in Action (p. 69)

1. Three types of spiritual meat are: 1) obedience, 2) deep truths in God's Word, and 3) Christ's Word.

2. In the story of the Good Samaritan, the Samaritan was performing the meat of the Lord, while the Levite and the priest did not perform the meat of the Lord. The obedience that was performed was love, because we are commanded to love our neighbor as ourselves.

3. There is hope for those who do not (obey) perform the meat of the Lord. In the story the prodigal son: 1) came back to the father, and 2) asked for forgiveness. The father was ready to forgive, and our heavenly Father is even more ready to forgive.

Gospel

Lesson 8

Prayer: Pray before each activity. Ask the Father for His Spirit to guide the minds of the students to learn more about Him and their Savior, Jesus Christ.

Activity 1

Noticing Sin in Nature

Take a walk in nature and point out to the students how the leaves die in the fall or how a flower dies when it is picked. These are results of sin. The beauty of nature reminds us of God's love, but the death in nature reminds us of sin. Romans 3:23 tells us, "The wages of sin is death but the gift of God is eternal life through Jesus Christ our Lord." There is a way out of death and that is through Christ Jesus. This is the gospel. Christ died for us and took the punishment that we deserve.

Activity 2

Missing the Mark

Items needed: suction cup "bullets," dry erase marker or masking tape, and a paper airplane

On a window or mirror make a target with a dry erase marker and have kids shoot the suction cups at the target trying to hit the bull's eye. You can also use masking tape to make a target on the floor and use paper airplanes to hit the bull's eye. Every time the child misses the bull's eye yell out "short." Give each child at least three turns to hit the mark and with each miss yell "short."

Ask the students:

- **How is this activity related to Biblical truth?** *Answer*: All have sinned and missed the mark. Romans 3:23: "For all have sinned, and come short of the glory of God."

- **What does it mean when the Bible says, "Come short of?"** *Answer*: we have sinned and have come short of being like Christ.

- **Because you have come short or sinned, what should happen to you?** *Answer*: We should die. Romans 6:23: "For the wages of sin is death; but the gift of God is eternal life through Jesus Christ our Lord."

- **What is the hope that is given in Romans 6:23?** *Answer*: God has given us a gift of eternal life by Jesus taking our punishment. 1 Peter 1:18, 19: "Forasmuch as ye know that ye were not redeemed with corruptible things, as silver and gold, from your vain conversation received by tradition from your fathers; But with the precious blood of Christ, as of a lamb without blemish and without spot."

- For those who hit the bulls eye, talk with them there are times in our life where victory is seen. There are times when people see Jesus in us. Ask children what that would look to see Jesus in others. Answer: kind words, helping someone who is sick or without food, praying or singing to someone. Tell the children that we are promised victory in Jesus.

Activity 3

Mark and Reflection

Items Needed: Mirror, washable markers, or face paint

Ask for at least two volunteers, who are willing to have marker or face paint put on their face. If you have more volunteers, then great.

1. Instruct those who did not volunteer not to say anything to the volunteers about what is on their faces.

2. You want to separate the volunteers where they can't see what you are doing to each one.

3. With marker or face paint put a dot or two on their face. Before you do this (without the child seeing) paint several of your fingers with the paint or marker so that when you touch their face it will come off your finger and onto their face without them knowing. This is done by touching their face as you are placing the other one or two dots on their face. This is done for each child.

4. Then you are going to instruct each volunteer to stand in front of the other non-volunteers. Remind the rest of the group to not say anything about the volunteers' faces.

5. As each volunteer comes out, tell them not to say anything about the other volunteers' faces, either.

Once all the volunteers are lined up ask each one the following question.

How many marks do you have on your face?

Once each volunteer has had an opportunity to answer give them the mirror and ask them the question again. **How many marks do you have on your face?**

The students will probably be surprised to see more than 2 marks on their face because they would have only felt you putting 1 or 2. Explain that they needed the mirror to really see more clearly how dirty their face actually was.

Have a volunteer read 1 Peter 1:18, 19 and ask the following questions.

- **What do you think the marks on your face represent?** *Answer*: Sin

- **What do you think the mirror represents?** *Answer*: law, Ten Commandments (Rom. 5:13; 7:7)

- **We read in Peter that Christ took our punishment so we could have life. This is the gospel, right?** *Answer*: Yes

- **Is that the end of the gospel?** *Answer*: No—if it was then Christ should have been able to come back for us already.

- **What is the target we are trying to hit in life?** *Answer*: to be like Christ, 2 Corinthians 3:18. We learned that the Ten Commandments are a symbol for Christ. When we look at those commandments, we should see Jesus' life. The more we look at His life represented by those commandments, we will want to follow His example and be more like Him.

- **What is another aspect of the gospel that has not been accomplished yet?** *Answer*: Christ represented fully in His people (Rom. 8:1–4)

Conclusion: Sin is a blemish and what shows us that blemish is the law, which is like a mirror. Christ's death paid the price for that blemish of sin. The gospel says that the Lord made us free from death, but He wants to make us free from sin also by looking to Him and His life.

More to the Gospel

Match the correct letter with the appropriate number to complete the thought.

____	1. The gospel of Christ is the image of ____. (2 Corinthians 4:4, 6)	a. child
____	2. The gospel of Christ is the power of God unto ____. (Romans 1:16)	b. Spirit
____	3. God asks us to be ____. (1 Peter 1:15, 16)	c. God
____	4. Part of the gospel is that the law would be fulfilled in ____. (Romans 8:2–4)	d. salvation
____	5. We can overcome by the ____. (Galatians 5:22–25)	e. us
____	6. The Spirit is also the ____. (John 6:63)	f. thoughts
____	7. Part of the gospel is that we can be a ____ of the King. (Galatians 4:6, 7)	g. holy
____	8. The mission is to be like Christ in our actions and our ____. (Philippians 2:5)	h. word

Multiple Choice

Known by Love

1. The purpose of the gospel of victory is _____. (Matt. 5:16)

    a. So that we can be perfect in order to live in heaven.
    b. Given so that others will see the change in our life and want to know Christ.
    c. Both of the above.
    d. None of the above.

2. The gospel of victory will _____. (John 17:23)

    a. Help us to know that God loves us.
    b. Bring us into unity with Christ and the Father.
    c. Draw us to love our Maker more.
    d. All of the above

3. The righteous man never sins. (Prov. 24:16)

    a. True
    b. False

4. The difference between the righteous and the wicked is the righteous never give up. (Prov. 24:16)

    a. True
    b. False

5. The world will see that we know God by _____ (Titus 1:14–6; John 13:35; 8:31; 15:8)

    a. Obeying the commandments.
    b. Our love for one another.
    c. Reading and following the word of God.
    d. Having the fruit of the Spirit.
    e. All of the above.

6. We learned that the law is the gospel, the gospel of Christ's perfect life. The other part of the gospel is that the Lord will not come until the law is fulfilled in us. (Matt. 5:18)

    a. True
    b. False

Metal Tooling

Materials: dull pencil with an eraser, image of the commandments, tape, 8½ x 11 cardstock paper (multiple colors), newspaper, 8½ x 11 heavy duty aluminum foil, glue

Procedure:

1. Fold newspaper several times to make a thick padded surface.
2. Tape aluminum foil shiny side down on newspaper.
3. Cut along dotted line to remove the text portion from the commandments clip art.
4. Place provided stencil of commandments on the foil and tape on the foil. Make sure you place the stencil towards the bottom portion of the foil to leave enough head space to put the Bible text at the top.
5. Use dull pencil to trace the stencil, using smooth strokes, being careful not to puncture the foil.
6. Once the commandments have been transferred, remove the paper.
7. With your dull pencil, lightly go over the trace marks directly on the foil, making sure you do not puncture the foil. This will give more definition to your image.
8. Remove the tape, turn the foil right side up, and place it on the cardstock, wrapping the excess foil around the edges of the cardstock. Secure the foil with tape or glue.
9. With your fingertip, smooth any unwanted lines, making sure not to touch the raised surfaces.
10. Take the 2 Corinthians 3:18 verse, cut the text to the desired size, and glue on a colored piece of cardstock.
11. Cut the desired design around the text and glue at the top of the commandments, in the extra space left from the stenciling.

Remind students that the law is a mirror or what the Bible calls a glass. We learned that Christ is also the law. The more we look at the law, the more we will see Christ's life. The more we look at this mirror, the more we will be changed into our Lord's image.

"But we all, with open face beholding as in a glass the glory of the Lord, are changed into the same image from glory to glory, even as by the Spirit of the Lord" (2 Corinthians 3:18)

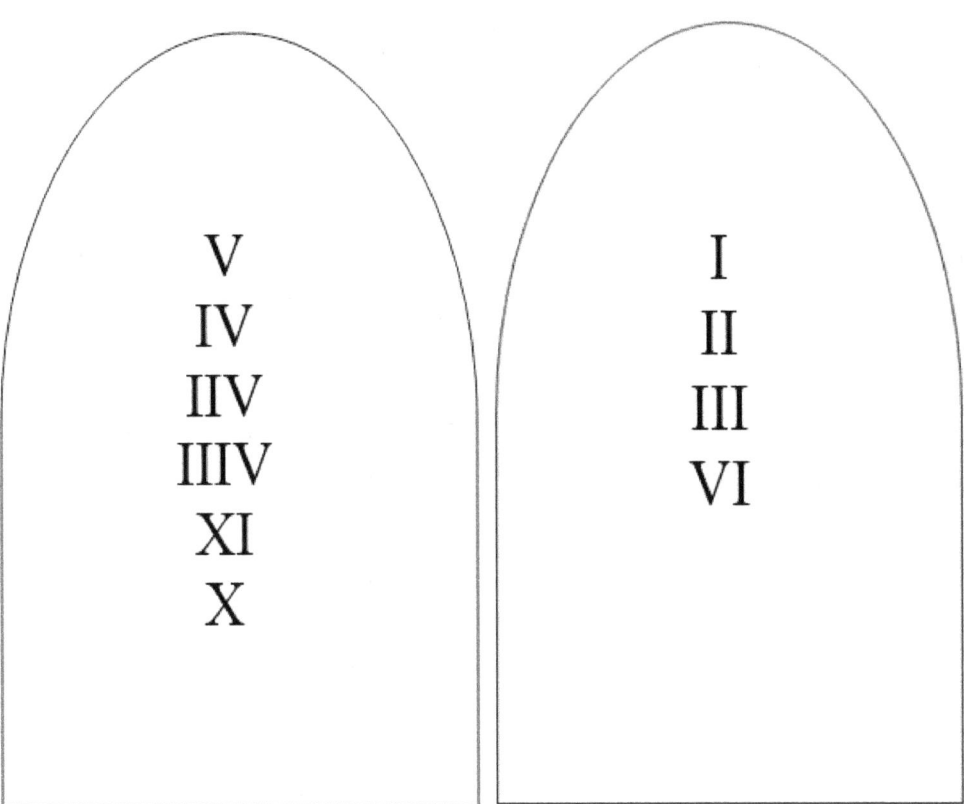

Answer Key for Lesson 8

More to the Gospel (p. 77)

1. C
2. D
3. G
4. E
5. B
6. H
7. A
8. F

Known by Love (p. 78)

1. B
2. D
3. B
4. A
5. E
6. A

TEACH Services, Inc.
P U B L I S H I N G

We invite you to view the complete
selection of titles we publish at:
www.TEACHServices.com

We encourage you to write us
with your thoughts about this,
or any other book we publish at:
info@TEACHServices.com

TEACH Services' titles may be purchased in
bulk quantities for educational, fund-raising,
business, or promotional use.
bulksales@TEACHServices.com

Finally, if you are interested in seeing
your own book in print, please contact us at:
publishing@TEACHServices.com
We are happy to review your manuscript at no charge.

www.ingramcontent.com/pod-product-compliance
Lightning Source LLC
Chambersburg PA
CBHW082232180426
43200CB00037B/2841